THIS NOTEBOOK BELONGS TO

FIRE LEGEND

The story of Manabozho, the Chippewa trickster hero who disguised himself as a shivering rabbit to steal fire from an old man's daughters, unfolds in this warmly colored pattern of hearth fires, combs, and shawls.

Pendleton Woolen Mills has been producing wool blankets in its Northwest American mills since 1909. Founded in 1863, this six-generation, family-owned business is renowned for world-class wool textiles in plaids, tweeds, bold stripes, and geometric patterns inspired by Native American artistic traditions. As its offerings have grown to include home, apparel, and accessories, Pendleton Woolen Mills has become synonymous with classic American style.

Copyright © 2019 by Pendleton Woolen Mills, Inc.

All rights reserved. No part of this product may be reproduced in any form without written permission from the publisher.

ISBN 978-1-4521-7251-4

Manufactured in China

10 9 8 7 6 5 4 3

Design by Kayla Ferriera

From *The Art of Pendleton Notebook Collection* published by Chronicle Books in 2019.

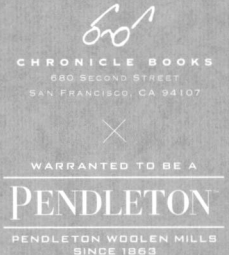

NOTEBOOK

THIS NOTEBOOK BELONGS TO

CRATER LAKE STRIPE

This design was created to honor the beauty of Crater Lake National Park. Colors of an Oregon sunset form a striped border against the dark blue waters of Crater Lake, formed in the caldera of an extinct volcano.

Pendleton Woolen Mills has been producing wool blankets in its Northwest American mills since 1909. Founded in 1863, this six-generation, family-owned business is renowned for world-class wool textiles in plaids, tweeds, bold stripes, and geometric patterns inspired by Native American artistic traditions. As its offerings have grown to include home, apparel, and accessories, Pendleton Woolen Mills has become synonymous with classic American style.

Copyright © 2019 by Pendleton Woolen Mills, Inc.

All rights reserved. No part of this product may be reproduced in any form without written permission from the publisher.

ISBN 978-1-4521-7251-4

Manufactured in China

10 9 8 7 6 5 4 3

Design by Kayla Ferriera

From *The Art of Pendleton Notebook Collection* published by Chronicle Books in 2019.

THIS NOTEBOOK BELONGS TO

GRAND CANYON PLAID

This pattern was introduced to celebrate the 100th anniversary of the National Park Service. The mile-deep geology of Arizona's Grand Canyon unfolds in a warm plaid of burnt umber, ochre, rust, and red against a deep blue background of sky and shadow.

Pendleton Woolen Mills has been producing wool blankets in its Northwest American mills since 1909. Founded in 1863, this six-generation, family-owned business is renowned for world-class wool textiles in plaids, tweeds, bold stripes, and geometric patterns inspired by Native American artistic traditions. As its offerings have grown to include home, apparel, and accessories, Pendleton Woolen Mills has become synonymous with classic American style.

Copyright © 2019 by Pendleton Woolen Mills, Inc.

All rights reserved. No part of this product may be reproduced in any form without written permission from the publisher.

ISBN 978-1-4521-7251-4

Manufactured in China

10 9 8 7 6 5 4 3

Design by Kayla Ferriera

From *The Art of Pendleton Notebook Collection* published by Chronicle Books in 2019.